First World War
and Army of Occupation
War Diary
France, Belgium and Germany

16 DIVISION
48 Infantry Brigade
Cameronians (Scottish Rifles)
18th Battalion
1 August 1918 - 28 February 1919

WO95/1975/7

The Naval & Military Press Ltd
www.nmarchive.com
Published in association with The National Archives

Published by

The Naval & Military Press Ltd

Unit 10 Ridgewood Industrial Park,

Uckfield, East Sussex,

TN22 5QE England

Tel: +44 (0) 1825 749494

www.naval-military-press.com

www.nmarchive.com

This diary has been reprinted in facsimile from the original. Any imperfections are inevitably reproduced and the quality may fall short of modern type and cartographic standards.

© **Crown Copyright**
Images reproduced by permission of The National Archives, London, England, 2015.

Contents

Document type	Place/Title	Date From	Date To
Heading	1975/7 18 Battalion Cameronians (Scottish Rifles) Aug 1918-Feb 1919		
Heading	16th Division 48th Infy Bde 18th Bn Scottish Rifles. Aug 1918-Feb 1919		
Heading	War Diary 18th Scottish Rifles. 1st August 1918 to 31st August 1918. Vol. I.		
War Diary	Boulogne	01/08/1918	16/08/1918
War Diary	Menneville	16/08/1918	22/08/1918
War Diary	Barlin	23/08/1918	29/08/1918
War Diary	Noeux-Les-Mines.	30/08/1918	31/08/1918
Miscellaneous	O.C. 18th Sco Rifles. H.Qrs 48th Inf Bde	02/10/1918	02/10/1918
Heading	War Diary 18th Scottish Rifles-B.E.F. 1st September 1918. to 30th September 1918 Volume II		
War Diary	Right Hohenzollern Sector, Right Sub Sectors.	01/09/1918	07/09/1918
War Diary	Annequin	08/09/1918	11/09/1918
War Diary	Hohenzollern.	12/09/1918	15/09/1918
War Diary	Reserve Posts	16/09/1918	17/09/1918
War Diary	Noeux-Les-Mines	18/09/1918	27/09/1918
War Diary	Cambrin	28/09/1918	30/09/1918
War Diary	Cambrin Sector Reserve	01/10/1918	03/10/1918
War Diary	Support	04/10/1918	04/10/1918
War Diary	Forward	05/10/1918	07/10/1918
War Diary	Forward Posts	08/10/1918	09/10/1918
War Diary	Annequin	10/10/1918	18/10/1918
War Diary	Camphin	19/10/1918	24/10/1918
War Diary	Wachemy	25/10/1918	03/11/1918
War Diary	Sentier	04/11/1918	05/11/1918
War Diary	Taintignies	06/11/1918	11/11/1918
War Diary	Antoing	12/11/1918	15/11/1918
War Diary	Genech	16/11/1918	16/11/1918
War Diary	Capelle	17/11/1918	30/11/1918
Miscellaneous	Report By O.C. 18th Battn. The Scottish Rifles on the part taken by the Battalion in the operations of 7.11.18 to 11.11.18	07/11/1918	07/11/1918
Heading	18th Scottish Rifles. War Diary From 1-12-18 to 31-12-18 Volume III		
War Diary	Cappelle	01/12/1918	31/01/1919
Heading	18th Scottish Rifles War Diary 1st February to 28th February 1919 SR/102 Vol 7		
War Diary	Cappelle	01/02/1919	28/02/1919

1925/4

18 Battalion Cameronians
(Scottish Rifles)

Aug 1916 — Feb 1919.

16TH DIVISION
48TH INFY BDE

18TH BN SCOTTISH RIFLES.
AUG 1918-FEB 1919

From U.K.

War Diary.

18th Scottish Rifles.

1st August 1918.   to   31st August 1918.

to
Feb '19

Vol. I.

Army Form C. 2118.

WAR DIARY OF 18th Sco. RIF.
or INTELLIGENCE SUMMARY
for AUGUST 1918

(Erase heading not required.)

Instructions regarding War Diaries and Intelligence Summaries are contained in F.S. Regs., Part II. and the Staff Manual respectively. Title pages will be prepared in manuscript.

Place	Date	Hour	Summary of Events and Information	Remarks and references to Appendices
BOULOGNE	1/8/18		The 18th Scottish Rifles left BOULOGNE by train for SAMER, and proceeded thence by route march to MENNEVILLE (Ref CALAIS 13. 4.E.40.20) where all ranks were billeted by 6 p.m.	
— do —	2/8/18		To-day was spent in "settling in", bathing, and cleaning up generally.	
— do —	3/8/18		Training commenced to-day, chiefly 'platoon' & section work. P.T. & B.F. started for N.C.Os.	
"	4/8/18		Nine signallers sent on a 6 weeks course. Special class in P.T. & B.F. started for N.C.Os.	
"	Aug. 5		Four miles route march to-day. H.Q. Coy. formed.	
"	6.		Training continues. Fatigue parties are out on all the training grounds, putting them in order.	
"	7.		Brigade Route March of 6½ miles. A tactical scheme, embracing the action of an advance guard on meeting a hostile force, was carried out	
"	8.		Reorganisation of "platoons" into 2 rifle sections and 1 double Lewis Gun section. Owing to shortage of men there are only 2 platoons per Coy.	
"	9.		Coy. training — an attack on a Machine Gun nest. Brigade Commander holds a conference with C.O. and Coy. Commanders to discuss an outpost scheme.	
"	10.		The Batt. carried out the Outpost Scheme discussed at Conference the previous day.	
"	11.		Church Parades.	
"	12 & 13		Platoon training special attention paid to "The Platoon in Attack" and "Reinforcing a platoon". Inspection of Transport by O.C. Divisional Train and by O.C. 145th Coy. A.S.C.	
"	14		The Battalion took part to-day in a Brigade Scheme acting as advanced guard to a force in pursuit of a retreating enemy. Great stress was laid on maintaining communication and the scouts were made full use of.	
"	15.		To-day was spent in bathing at DESVRES and firing practice on 500x range.	
"	16.		Parades as usual in the morning while in the afternoon all ranks attended a lecture on "Bayonet fighting" by Lt-Col Campbell, Deputy Instructor of P. & B.T.	

Army Form C. 2118.

WAR DIARY
or
INTELLIGENCE SUMMARY
(Erase heading not required.)

Instructions regarding War Diaries and Intelligence Summaries are contained in F.S. Regs., Part II. and the Staff Manual respectively. Title pages will be prepared in manuscript.

Place	Date	Hour	Summary of Events and Information	Remarks and references to Appendices
MENNEVILLE	Aug 14		Owing out of the Inspector of Infantry's Report the duty of Orderly Sergeant is done away with. Warning Order received from 148 Bde. re relief of 1st Division by 16th Division	
"	17.		Capt. J.B. Hamilton proceeded to-day to 1st Army Infantry Course at HARDELOT. Court of Enquiry held to inquire into case of absentees when 16th Division left U.K.	
"	18.		Church Parades: Our 2/Lt. Spreckley to VIII Corps Gas School. 2/Lt. Howard to III and Army School of Scouting and 3 men to a Course in Signal work with pigeons. Batt. Sports were held to-day, No. 3 Coy. winning the Coy. Competition by a large number of points.	
"	19.		Handed in to-day in preparation for move to BARLIN in all Training Stores detailed orders for which were received to-day.	
"	20.		The 1st Corps area, and Coy Commander proceeded in advance to BARLIN to-day the Commanding Officer along with the 49th & 52nd Bde.	
"	21.		All preparations completed for to-morrows move. Transport proceeds to-day.	
"	22.		The Battalion entrained at DESVRES to-day at 8.30 a.m. and proceeded to BARLIN there relieving the a' Batt. of the 49th Inf. Bde. in Divisional Reserve. C.O. 2nd in Command	
BARLIN	23		To-day was spent chiefly in bathing and cleaning parades. Specialist Officers and Transport arrived to-night.	
"	24		Training all day. Specialist under Specialist Officers, and remainder of Battalion practicing patrolling. C.O., 2nd in Command, Coy Commander & Intelligence Officer reconnoitred area between NOEUX-LES-MINES and SAILLY-LA-BOURSE. Draft of 107 men arrived to-night	
"	25		Church Parades. Platoon Officers reconnoitred area between NOEUX-LES-MINES and SAILLY LA BOURSE. Brig. General inspected the draft, addressing them on their duties & responsibilities.	

Army Form C. 2118.

WAR DIARY
or
INTELLIGENCE SUMMARY.
(Erase heading not required.)

Instructions regarding War Diaries and Intelligence Summaries are contained in F. S. Regs., Part II. and the Staff Manual respectively. Title pages will be prepared in manuscript.

Place	Date	Hour	Summary of Events and Information	Remarks and references to Appendices
BARLIN	26 Aug		The Battalion was on the 300 yd range at REBREUVE from 6 a.m. to 3 p.m. Musketry instruction was given. A Platoon exercise carried out during intervals of waiting.	
do.	27		Specialist training during forenoon. At night the Battalion assembled in position to be occupied by 'C' Battalion in case of attack in recent line between NOEUX-LES-MINES and SAILLY LA BOURSE (as a practise.)	
do.	28		The Battalion is now attached to 47th Inf. Bde pending the time when the 5th Royal Irish Fus. will be fit for the line. The C.O, Coy. Commanders, L.G.O and Intelligence Officer reconnoitre B Reserve Batt. area	
do.	29		Today the Battalion proceeded to NOEUX-LES-MINES & took over the camp of the 5th Royal Irish Fus. observing on the way a S.O.S. demonstration	
NOEUX-LES-MINES	30		Reconnaissance by C.O & Coy Commanders of Right Battalion front. Advance party consisting of L.G.O Intelligence Officer O1 officer per Coy, No 1 of the Lewis Gun teams & Batt. observers proceed to trenches in Right Batt. Sector of Right	
do.	31.		The Battalion relieved the 14th Leicester in Right Batt. Sector of Right Brigade front.	

James Peebie Major
Comdg 18 Scottish Rifles.

MEMORAN[DUM]

BM32

From O.C.
18th Scot Rifles.

To H.Qrs.
48th Inf. Bde.

2-10-18   191

Herewith War Diary for month of September 1918. Please acknowledge receipt hereof.

W. L. Heath
2/Lt & Adjt.
for O.C. 18th S.R.

War Diary

18ᵀᴴ Scottish Rifles — B.E.F.

1ˢᵀ September 1918.
to.
30ᵀᴴ September 1918.

Volume II

WAR DIARY or INTELLIGENCE SUMMARY

Army Form C. 2118.

(Erase heading not required.)

Place	Date	Hour	Summary of Events and Information	Remarks and references to Appendices
RIGHT HOHEN-ZOLLERN SECTOR	Sep.1.		Our front was quiet during the day. The men were engaged in repairing trenches and strengthening defences.	
RIGHT SUB SEC-TOR.	2.	3 p.m.	Patrols from all Coys. sent out to reconnoitre enemy positions with order to occupy such if no enemy found. Patrols returned on finding enemy positions occupied. Battle patrols pushed forward and met with heavy machine gun fire. On returning 1 man was found missing. 1 prisoner captured by no. 4 Coys patrol.	
	3		Patrols out day and night to keep touch with enemy, and to report any signs of them retiring.	
	4. 5. 6.		Patrols still active. 2/Lt. J.W. BARTLE wounded. Three Coys. push forward and establish posts, but on the Battalion on our left being forced back two of these Coys. withdrew to original positions, No.1. Coy. still holding on. 2/Lt. R.T. REID gassed.	
	7	7 A.M.	No.1. Coy. ordered to withdraw to original position at ANNEQUIN.	
ANNEQUIN	8		The Battalion on relief by 14th Leicesters proceeded to ANNEQUIN, leaving No.1 Coy in VILLAGE LINE.	
"	9		Day spent in cleaning up and bathing.	
"	10		Parades including tactical schemes, wiring and specialist training.	
"	11		Parades as for 10th inst. No 2 Coy relieved No.1 Coy in VILLAGE LINE.	
HOHENZOLLERN.	12.		The Battalion relieved the 14th Leicesters in Right Sub Sector. Working on a prisoner's statement of enemy retirement, No. 1 & 2 Coys were sent forward to establish posts at 4 p.m. followed by 3 & 4 Coys. who passed through them and established posts round FOSSE 8.	

Army Form C. 2118.

WAR DIARY
or
INTELLIGENCE SUMMARY.

(Erase heading not required.)

Place	Date	Hour	Summary of Events and Information	Remarks and references to Appendices
HOHENZOLLERN	Sept 13		Battalion H.Q. moved to advanced position at EVENING POST at dawn. Our forward posts heavily bombarded with H.E. and Gas shells. A considerable number of casualties mainly from the latter resulting. Battle Patrol went forward to clear top of FOSSE 8 of snipers. The 14th Leicester occupied all positions left by Battalion on its going forward.	
do.	14.		All positions held. Visual Signalling station established on FOSSE 8 to L.2 Post from which communication was available to Batt. H.Q. A similar station was established on FOSSE 8 to ANNEQUIN FOSSE. Forward post heavily shelled with H.E. and Yellow X during the night. 4D Casualties resulting, including 2/Lt. MACKINNON, HEPPLE, BIRD, and STARK, gassed.	
do.	15.		Battalion relieved by 14th Leicester. Coys took up positions at CENTRAL KEEP, BARTS POST, SUSSEX POST (SURBITON). Approximately 40 casualties reported chiefly gas.	
RESERVE POSTS	16.		Baths at ANNEQUIN. CENTRAL KEEP heavily shelled from 6-7 p.m. with 5.9. Approximately 50 men Casualties (gas).	
	17.		Baths at ANNEQUIN. 2/Lt. KIRKWOOD gassed.	
NOEUX-LES-MINES	18.		The Battalion proceeded to NOEUX-LES-MINES and took over billets and duties of 5th Royal Irish Fusiliers. Capt. W.C. FRASER sent to 6th C.C.S. (Gassed.)	
do.	19.		Day spent in clearing up, refitting, reorganizing etc.	
do.	20.		Training parades. Practice in battle patrols and attacking strong points. Lectures by platoon officers on "mopping up".	
do.	21.		Training parades during forenoon. In the evening the Battalion marched to BARLIN to attend Concert by Divisional troupe, "The Blackthorns".	

Army Form C. 2118.

WAR DIARY
INTELLIGENCE SUMMARY.
(Erase heading not required.)

Place	Date	Hour	Summary of Events and Information	Remarks and references to Appendices
NOEUX-LES-MINES	Sept. 22		Church Parade. Battalion inspected by Commanding Officer.	
do.	23.		Training parades and practice in wiring. Draft of 27 other ranks arrived to-day.	
do.	24.		Range practices and musketry lectures by Platoon Commanders. 6 Officers (reinforcements) from U.K. joined for duty to-day. G.O.C. 48th Inf Bde visited the Camp to-day.	
do.	25		Additional Lewis Gun teams in Training. Battalion almost wholly engaged on Guards and Fatigues.	
do.	26		Training as usual.	
do.	27		Battalion relieved the 3rd K.R.R. in CAMBRIN area, becoming Reserve Battalion of Brigade in Line. Working party of 90 men on forward posts. N.C.Os. course instruction from Brigade Gas Officer. Working party at AUCHY.	
CAMBRIN	28		Training in musketry, wiring and patrolling (by night)	
do	29		Training in musketry. Working parties of 100 ORs on work of front posts	
do	30		Carrying and working parties. Strob captain of 1 strong trench 24 hours check through in at midnight 30/1st Oct.	

Armitage Lt Col
Comdg 18 Sea. Rifles.

WAR DIARY or INTELLIGENCE SUMMARY

Army Form C. 2118.

18th (S) BATTALION ORDERLY ROOM 1 NOV 1918 THE SCOTTISH RIFLES

Place	Date	Hour	Summary of Events and Information	Remarks and references to Appendices
CAMBRAI SECTOR RESERVE	Oct 1.		The Batt. is now Reserve Batt. of Brigade in line. 22nd N.F's read forward and we take up positions at LEWIS KEEP. CAMBRIN heavily shelled from 15.30 to 17.15.	
do	2		Battalion again moves forward. H.Q. at ROBERTSON'S TUNNEL.	
do	3		Enemy still retiring so Batt. pushes forward H.Q. to AUCHY and Coys. to CITÉ DOUVRIN and HAISNES. Capt Habok goes to Div. Reception Camp owing to sprained ankle. Lt COULTER & 2/Lt PAUL posted on course at 1 Corps School. Draft of 27 O.R arrives posted to No 2 Coy.	
SUPPORT	4		Coys move to support positions in DOUVRIN area. Batt. H.Q being situated in CITÉ DOUVRIN.	
FORWARD	5		Batt. relieves 22 N.F. in forward positions with Batt. H.Q. at BILLY BERCLAU. Disposition – 2 Coys in forward posn, 1 Coy in support at BERCLAU and 1 Coy. in BILLY BERCLAU. Patrols:- No. 1 Coy established post with 2 platoons on W. bank of Canal but one of these was withdrawn owing to swampy nature of ground & heavy M.G. fire. No. 3 b Coy sent out reconnoitring patrol. No. 2 Coy (support) relieved No 4 Coy in posn.	
do	6		Patrols: 2 Officers and 14 O.R. of No 3 Coy (2/Lt MANNES in Command) attacked M.G. post at O.13.c.45.06 at 23.00. three rows of wire found had to be cut with wire cutters. Patrol got to within 12 yards of sentry before being seen. Our rushed the position (a house) and found 10 Germans in a room. Our escaped, eight killed and one captured and brought back. Patrol returned having 2 casualties. 2/Lt MANNES & C.S.M. WILLIAMS slightly wounded.	
do	7		No 3 Coy relieved No 2 Coy.	

WAR DIARY or INTELLIGENCE SUMMARY.

Army Form C. 2118.

Place	Date	Hour	Summary of Events and Information	Remarks and references to Appendices
FORWARD POSTS	Oct 8		Forward area heavily shelled.	
do	9		Acting on a prisoners statement that the enemy was preparing a daylight patrol in BILLY BERCLAU - CANAL ROAD. Patrol met with heavy hostile M.G. fire during which 2/Lt FULTON, C.S.M WILLIAMS and 1 O.R. were killed. The Batt. was relieved by 1st Leicesters by 23.00. Heavy hostile shelling during relief. Coys proceeded by motor lorry from HAISNES to ANNEQUIN VILLAGE coy Batt. H.Q. in FOSSE.	
ANNEQUIN	10.		Day spent in bathing, cleaning equipment, clothing and rifle inspections. Batt of 13 O.R. posted to no. 2 Coy.	
do.	11.		Coy Parades - Platoons with Platoon Commander. Specialist training in afternoon.	
do.	12.		Coys at disposal of O.C. Coys - movement in open warfare - advanced flank and rear guards - route march. Lewis Gunners training all day under R.E. instructors.	
do.	13		200 men supplied as working party to R.E. for salvage of Iron Rations at Church Parade held at the FOSSE.	
do.	14		Battalion Scheme. 2 Coys marching from direction of NOEUX-LES-MINES and clearing enemy (2 Coys) rearguard from TOURBIERES (marching along NOYELLES - CAMBRIN Road))	
do.	15		Demonstration given by no 4 Coy in use of Ground Flares with Contact Aeroplane. Warning received that Batt. might move forward in view of expected further enemy retirement on Divisional front.	

WAR DIARY
or
INTELLIGENCE SUMMARY

(Erase heading not required.)

Army Form C. 2118.

18th (S) BATTALION
ORDERLY ROOM
7 NOV 1918
THE SCOTTISH RIFLES

Place	Date	Hour	Summary of Events and Information	Remarks and references to Appendices
	Oct 16		Batt. moves forward Coys to LEWIS, PYRENEES, SUSSEX and TOWERS POSTS, and Bn. H.Q. to ROBERTSON'S TUNNEL. Major HG CRAWFORD, 13th Royal Scots reports for duty and takes up position of 2nd in Command.	
	17		Batt. including transport and Q.M. Stores move to BERCLAU. By further orders march was continued to PROVIN. A day of heavy marching.	
	18		Batt. marched to CAMPHIN via ANNOEULIN move being completed & battalion billeted by 12.00. Several civilians found in village.	
CAMPHIN	19		Draft of 21 O.R. arrived. 2/Lt H. ROBINSON from 11 Hants(?) reports for duty and is posted to "A" Coy. 4 O.R. accidentally injured by explosion at H.Q. billet.	
	20		Battalion moved to AVELIN. Inspection of Iron Rations in all Coys. Piquets were posted at roads entering village to prevent undue movement of civilians between villages. The Commanding Officer acted as Commandant of the village and the local Maire was under his jurisdiction.	
	21		March continued to HARDINIÈRE via ENNEVELINT, LE PARADIS, Batt. H.Q. being at A.16.a.30.60 (Sheet 44 1/40,000 16th Division "Standa fast".	
	22		Training resumed. Lectures by Coy Commanders on wood patrolling & fighting.	
	23		Batt. H.Q. 3 & 4 Coys. Q.M. Stores moved to WACHEMY.	
	24		A working party of 250 O.R. was supplied for R.E. Dahque of road repairing in SENECH. Signalling was established with Bn. Hqs. at TEMPLEUVE.	
WACHEMY	25		Specialist training resumed.	

WAR DIARY.

Place.	Date.	Hour.	Summary of events and information.	Remarks and references to Appendices
WACHEMY	Oct. 27.		R.E. working party of 250 men supplied. Training as usual. Church Services held to-day. The village is patrolled nightly, it being suspected that enemy agents are prowling about.	
do.	28.		Battalion Scheme - "A (Hope consisting of 1 Battalion (less 1 Coy) has been in outpost position round GENECH district 28/29 Oct. On 29 the Bn. Commander intends to resume his march to PERONNE. From information received from a reliable civilian the presence of enemy in LA RUE at X 29.c.o.d is known & usual precautions are therefore to be taken during advance. Communication by all visual methods	
do.	29.		during advance. Communication by all visual methods practised.	
do.	30.		Coy. training. Extended order drill - practice in use of ground & cover - artillery formation. Specialist training continued.	
do.	31.		Working parties to number of 100 men engaged chiefly on road repair. Whole transport engaged conveying material for road repair. Coy. training. Visit of Divisional Commander.	

JCMStrutter Lt. Col.
Comdg. 18 Scottish Rifles

Army Form C. 2118.

18 Scottish Rifles
10 L 4

WAR DIARY
or
INTELLIGENCE SUMMARY.
(Erase heading not required.)

Instructions regarding War Diaries and Intelligence Summaries are contained in F.S. Regs., Part II. and the Staff Manual respectively. Title pages will be prepared in manuscript.

Place	Date	Hour	Summary of Events and Information	Remarks and references to Appendices
WACHERY	Nov 1		Training under Coy arrangements. Special classes for N.C.O.s in P.T. & B.F.	
"	2		Coy training including fire orders & fire control & Lethlem formations	
"	3		Major 2 Games, D.S.O. (Black Watch Royal) takes over command of the Battalion from Lt Col D.M. Stubbs who proceeded to-day to UK on 3 months leave. Battalion moves to SENTIER.	
SENTIER	4		Reconnaissance of position to be held by Battalion in case of a hostile break through. Brigade Commander's Conference with C.O.s followed by C.O's Conference with all officers to discuss probable operations. Coy training in [?]. Warning order received that Battalion will relieve 18 Gloucesters in Reserve on [?] next.	
	6		Batt. relieves Gloucesters as Reserve Bath of Brigade. See attached report.	
TAINTIGNIES	6			
	7-11		A, B Coys inspected by Commanding Officer. Officers class in "Rifle drill" it having been decided to introduce the drill of a Rifle Regiment into the Battalion.	
ANTOING	12			
	13		Inspection of C & D Coys by Commanding Officer. Kit inspection by Coy of every man on Coy Pay List.	
"	14		C.O's inspection of H.Q. personnel. Battn detailed to remove German signs and notices.	
"	15		Battalion proceeded to VELVAIN.	

Army Form C. 2118.

WAR DIARY
or
INTELLIGENCE SUMMARY.
(Erase heading not required.)

Instructions regarding War Diaries and Intelligence Summaries are contained in F. S. Regs., Part II. and the Staff Manual respectively. Title pages will be prepared in manuscript.

Place	Date	Hour	Summary of Events and Information	Remarks and references to Appendices
GENECH	NOV. 16		The Battalion proceeded by march route to GENECH dinner being served en route. Regimental Band accompanied.	
CAPELLE	17		The Batt. marched to CAPELLE which is likely to be our location for an indefinite period.	
"	18		Practice in "Rifle" drill continued. Sports Committee formed. Platoon training continues.	
"	19 20 21		Arrangements made for collecting vegetables from neighbouring fields. Education classes under Capt. Hamilton and Platoon football competition in full swing.	
"	22 23		Baths & delousing of blankets at TEMPLEUVE LILLE granted Battalion Leave for officers to visit & stay overnight in LILLE. "Night Out"s at "BLACKTHORNS", TEMPLEUVE	
"	24 25		Ordish services. Inspection of transport by Commanding Officer. Areas allotted to Companies for keeping roads in repair, removal of German notices, collection of vegetables & salvage purposes.	
"	26 27 28		Training football Bayonet v. Optima dens (26 inst) Education classes as usual. Sort of divisional training interrupted by rain.	
"	29 30		Work on above of battn proceeding steadily. Great increase in attendance at Education Classes.	

1st Bn. Leinster Regt
for Lt. Col. (illegible)
Commdt. 1st Bn Leinster Regt (illegible)

REPORT

by O.C. 18th Battn. The Scottish Rifles on the
part taken by the Battalion in the operations
of 7.11.18 to 11.11.18.

1. In accordance with 48th Inf. Bde. Order No. 41 dated 7.11.18, my No. 2 Coy. relieved a Coy. of the 5th Bn. R.I.Fus. in the Outpost Line at BRUYELLE (Area V.20.c.) and became the Brigade Right Front Company. This relief was completed at 04.10. on 8.11.18 when the Company came under the command of O.C. 5th Bn. R.I.Fus. and the relieved Coy. of 5th R.I. Fus. returned to billets at TAINTEGNIES and came under my command.

2. On the night of 8th/9th November 1918, in accordance with Brigade Order No. 43 dated 8.11.18, my Battalion (less 1 Coy. already in the line) relieved the three remaining Companies of the 5th Bn. R.I.Fus. in the line. While this relief was still in progress verbal orders were received from Brigade H.Q. that the left half of the line held by 5th R.I.Fus. would be relieved by the 22nd N.Fus. and that this latter Bn. together with my Battn. were to effect a crossing of the River SCHELDT during the night 8th/9th November 1918 and form a Bridge-head by holding the railway line, the boundaries of which so far as my Bn. was concerned were to be (Right) CHATEAU DE BRUYELLE V.26.b.1.9 (Left) V.20.b.7.9. - V.21.b.5.7. and thence along road to V.22.central. This necessitated a re-arrangement of the Battn. dispositions generally including side-slipping but this was accomplished very rapidly without confusion, and Bn. H.Q. established at OLD KILNS (V.20.c.2.7.).

3. My dispositions then were - 3 Coys (less two platoons) in front line, with one Coy. in support and two platoons of the centre front line Coy at Billet No. 38 BRUYELLE detailed to bring up and launch boats for the ordered crossing. During the night one section Field Coy. R.E., one section L.T.M.Battery and one section M.G.C. reported to me and placed themselves at my disposal.

4. Having previously conferred with and given orders to the Officers concerned, and having allotted their respective frontages and objectives, I thereupon ordered the crossing of the River to be commenced by three Coys., covered by the support Coy. which had meanwhile established itself in houses along the Riverside. As the 22nd N.Fus. had not at that time come up on my left flank I allotted one section L.T.M.B. with half-section M.G.C. to the support Coy and half section M.G.C. to my left front Coy. to strengthen that flank.

5. The 2½ Coys having advanced into position on the West bank of the River, my two platoons at BRUYELLE, assisted by one section F. Coy. R.E. brought up boats and the crossing of the SCHELDT was effected by my centre and left Coys. without opposition under the energetic and able direction of the R.E. Officers attached, and by my right Coy. over a temporary footbridge at V.26.c.2.7. The crossing was completed by 02.00. My casualties were - 1 O.R. drowned and 1 O.R. wounded.

6. After crossing the River, my three Coys. advanced without opposition to their allotted objectives and established Posts along the railway line from V.27.c.0.0. - V.22.a.3.7., the right Coy. gaining touch with the Division on our right and the left Coy. forming a defensive flank along the main road from V.21.c.5.7. - V.22.d.2.7. These positions were taken up by N.x.N. 04.00 and held until 16.00 on 9.11.18 when Coys. were withdrawn to billets in accordance with Brigade Order "B.M.91" dated 9.11.18.

7. In conclusion, the following points appear to me to be worthy of consideration in the training for, or (as the case may be) planning of future similar operations. -
   (a) Squads should be practiced in moving noiselessly over rough ground in the dark with heavy and bulky objects.
   (b) Night operations should include the crossing of Rivers, and by planks over cuttings and similar obstacles.
   (c) Boats or other bridging material could be placed or man-handled

into position noiselessly and with greater rapidity by using vehicles in the nature of (rubber tyred) wheeled stretchers.
(d) Rope attachments for haulage of boats across Rivers are more effective and efficient than the use of paddles.

11.11.18.
          Signed. F. EAVES, Lieut. Colonel,
          <u>Commanding 18th Scottish Rifles.</u>

18TH SCOTTISH RIFLES.

WAR DIARY

From 1-12-18 to 31-12-18

VOLUME III

Army Form C. 2118.

WAR DIARY
or
INTELLIGENCE SUMMARY.
(Erase heading not required.)

Instructions regarding War Diaries and Intelligence Summaries are contained in F. S. Regs., Part II. and the Staff Manual respectively. Title pages will be prepared in manuscript.

Place	Date	Hour	Summary of Events and Information	Remarks and references to Appendices
CAPPELLE	DEC 1		Church Parade. Concert this R.C.'s in CAPPELLE Church. SOR moved to UK depot HARRISTON (new works)	
	2		Baths and indent scrounging. Repair squad at work on Lititz. Shut Park to Army SOS School. 2 Shr Skpool from Base depot	
	3		M.O.C. Obtained billets and various permanent arrangements 10.15 arrive 10.15 in Billiard Institute (Pothers) Correspondence Started	
	4		P.T. and Games and Entertainment. 2 hut Services. At Sourceres. AFF Education dept Committee formed for Sports and entertainments	
	5		Band Practice CAPPELLE	
	6		Parades as usual. PONT-A-MOUSSON - LE PAUL-BERSEE-TOURS-CAPPELLE. Demobilisation explained to all & Coys by the CO in theatre Ine puppet theatre (?Nicten): 2 or from Podetta	
	7		Lecture for 60 ops and 20% at Tembene on "ALSACE-LORRAINE" Demobilisation Villages to 2 companies Jointly arranged by the Education dept.	
	8		Church Parade as usual. Band. Sunday evening entertainment	
	9		Parades usual. Sports in afternoon. Report to indicate Le THOUARS Commander. C.O's conference of Commanders. Report shews in short facts.	
10			Hilson fell all Candidates in Contact.	
11			Parade all ranks 10.45. 2 L.a.c. (nurses) 16 Disposal centre Martin Square in absence for Ceremonial drill followed by C.O's conference. EO - as soon Rines could	

WAR DIARY or INTELLIGENCE SUMMARY

Army Form C. 2118.

Place	Date	Hour	Summary of Events and Information	Remarks and references to Appendices
CAPPELLE	12.		Brigade removed Sunday. Battalion coming to include advance brigade. 14 OR (men) to U.K.	
	13.		Battn Sunday. Battalion Annual Rifle Meeting of Bgd SxR.15. 17 OR. (number to att.) (C' Coy. Lewis MG (1) & 3 Coy. 18.50 Rifles (ind.) on R&C Competition.	
	14.		Enlargement of Rifle (Lewis indr&c)	
	15.		Church Parade as usual. Rifle Coys commence one week "tour of duty." Parade daily Brookly Road. Lorry allotted to take officers and OR to Lille 2 half hour & 3-4 days.	
	16.		Bath Parade. Returns in rs Privates holding Leveau at TEMPLEUVE. 10.15 Platoon joins Higher competition.	
	17.		Battn Parade as or (minor) to U.K.	
	18.		Baths and minor leveaux. Pillows handed to men. Paillasses by Carpet Guard.	
	19.		Brigade loads remitted. Battn leveau held. Normal stores in readiness for men.	
	20.		Battn Parade. P.S.Z.H. expected for remission (y all ranks.)	
	21.		Battn Parade. 9 a.m 1,360 to R 500 R.M. (indr) am Divisional Competition	
	22.		Church Parade. Lunch service at CYSOING	
	23.		Battn Parade. Battn Leveau standard until 12.6. books. Company Commanders Conference	
	24.		Battn Parade. Rehearsal & readiness for 3 Runners	
	25.		Christmas day. Xmas dinners by OR. Performance by officers' party. Award. Awarding competition won by M.M. platoon "C" Coy.	
	26.		Holiday. Xmas at Battn.	
	27.		Baths at Templeuve. O.R. ledger to charge of Instruction (Education)	

Army Form C. 2118.

WAR DIARY
or
INTELLIGENCE SUMMARY.
(Erase heading not required.)

Instructions regarding War Diaries and Intelligence Summaries are contained in F. S. Regs., Part II. and the Staff Manual respectively. Title pages will be prepared in manuscript.

Place	Date	Hour	Summary of Events and Information	Remarks and references to Appendices
CAPELLE	28		Companies parade under Platoon Commanders in billets for Medical exam.	
	29		Church parade. Battalion moved party gave rehab performance. 2 O.R. to Medical centre.	
	30		Company training in a.m. Bullets 10 O.R. on salvage work at PERONNES.	
	31		Batt. parade. Sports competitions.	

_____ LIEUT. COLONEL
Commanding 18th Battn. The Scottish Rifles

Army Form C. 2118.

To H.Q. 2nd 48th Infy. Brigade /

1/8th (G) Batt. Scottish Rifles

WAR DIARY
or
INTELLIGENCE SUMMARY
(Erase heading not required.)

Instructions regarding War Diaries and Intelligence Summaries are contained in F.S. Regs. Part II. and the Staff Manual respectively. Title pages will be prepared in manuscript.

Place	Date	Hour	Summary of Events and Information	Remarks and references to Appendices
CAPPELLE	Jan 1918		The Ordinary Programme of Training 1918 Effected. Completion presented with Troops in Theatre. Captain Stewart exhibited fit of grip. etc.	
	2		Baths and Industry Economy. 2nd Lt. Ansth Mihorte A.Dmy. attached. 2nd Lt G.F. Mannock Active A. & I. Attached. Alfred Park attached to C.G.T. Coy temporarily.	
	3		Battalion bought two Films for Signalling on the Range. Captain Mason M.C. Photo Effect from T.F. H.Q.	
	4		Rifle reverts to the training duty of Regimental Records received and not utilisation of Regimental Customs of funerary for Church not yet.	
	5		Church Parade. R.C. at Dumpleine at 10.30 Other Denomination in the Theatre at 11.30. Other ranks took place in C.C. for this not seeing their of Quarters. They got Regimental souvenirs and spent 1 O.R's moved to forest Depot at 3 O.P.	
	6		Ordinary Parades resumed 7 O.R's and 1 O.M. Stores. Battalion is on duty parade at Bapaume and Dumpleine	
	7		Since the N.C.O.'s and O.R.'s at Dumpleine Effective at pickeye Sheafed Demolition to Exploit appeared. Wire of Front Strands to Finishing to Elephant Gate. Work was carried out by Reynaud Brigade Rangetype 1400-1600. Moves ankoor Drove Shrapnel & Lost in Shere	
	8		D Coy on Baths in Bully E Coy in Bully. 1st Lieut. Thouart the left Brigade morning ZEHN 136 O.R's at last Hammond	

Z.6

Army Form C. 2118.

WAR DIARY
or
INTELLIGENCE SUMMARY.
(Erase heading not required.)

Instructions regarding War Diaries and Intelligence Summaries are contained in F. S. Regs., Part II. and the Staff Manual respectively. Title pages will be prepared in manuscript.

Place	Date	Hour	Summary of Events and Information	Remarks and references to Appendices
CAPPELLE	Jan 1919 (Cont'd)			
	9th		1 other rank from Hospital	
	10th		Working Parties + Guards. Concert Party of N.F.'s in Theatre. "Colonial Development" Guards + Working Parties. Lecture at TEMPLEUVE at 1050 on Ashwell Concert Party @ 1400 hours. Lt. Col. Eeno on -10th 30 Yts. Rev Ashwell M.C. takes over Command	
	11th		Major Crawford M.C. takes over Command	
	12th		Church Services 11.45. C.E. CAPPELLE - 11.00 Pres Wes + R.C. @ CAPPELLE 3 Rinds Peelle 30 Yts to diocesan cadre. C.S.M. McMullin takes over duties of R.S.M. B. Coy. vs. vs. C. Coy. at football – result C- 2 goals; B - 1 goal.	
	13th		Coy. Command shoot made magistrate in Gun Stores hundred in flying Corps. Comedy by Boomerangs. (2nd Lieut. Australian) the Magistrate.	
	14th		3 Rinds O.R.s appointed temporary Sergeants. Officer from 13th Jaegers Company Parades Lord Stampfell on leave. 2nd Battn moves Signallers on holiday. "Boomerangs - 2nd Battn Batho. Italians verses 155 Coy R.E. at football Whist Drive at 18.00 hours at Bn HQ Rec Room.	
	15th		6 others Hamilton from leave Brunels Concert Party in Theatre at 18.00 hours.	
	16th		Brigade Sentry Exam. Pont à Marcq – Ennevelin – Seenhem CAPPELLE – approx 11 kilos - Rinds - 2 miles. Won by Private Roberts 20th Coy 2nd Bn. Cross Country Runners "B" 3rd Battalion – 2 miles 'B' Coy. Route Campbell B - 3rd Company Shyround 19/4/15 within Drama in Theatre.	
	17th		Orders issued for all men entitled to wear 1914/15 ribbon	

Army Form C. 2118.

WAR DIARY
or
INTELLIGENCE SUMMARY.
(Erase heading not required.)

Instructions regarding War Diaries and Intelligence Summaries are contained in F.S. Regs., Part II. and the Staff Manual respectively. Title pages will be prepared in manuscript.

Place	Date	Hour	Summary of Events and Information	Remarks and references to Appendices
CAPPELLE	Jan 18/19		Battalion Orders for Demobilisation of Battalion. 3 groups A Coy N.Fus. at TEMPLEUVE. — victry for So. Staffs. Battalion meat party in Theatre. End of	
	19th		Coy. Cup. against CAPPELLE. 5 O.R.s to Disposal Centre.	
	20th		2/Lieut. Young appointed Bgde Educational Officer with rank of a/Capt. from 5/1/19. Lecture December 25 O.R.s Amalgam. K.R.R. Cncnd party in Theatre.	
	21st		Coy. War Cppbal. with 22nd N.F.S. Call for men - 13 vyrs.	
	22nd		Drawing Programme. Lecture at TEMPLEUVE for 10 officers + 100 O.Rs. - interpret- ments on Staffs. Egypt + China. Coy Commanders Conference at 12.30. Capt. Sgt. ab 2/Lt Coulter. 20 D.Rs to Disposal Centre. Whapley Cup final Livestrhp verus R.I.F. 2 goals to 1	
	23rd		Battalion Route March. - Thoronat Bioaw Anchy Cappelle. Dance in Marie Templeuve. B. Coy. I.R. versus D. Coy. N.Fus. ment 3 goals nil.	
	24th		Lecture on Demobilisation in Theatre for C & D. Coys - by Capt. Hamilton. Coy A, B & C Coys. B. Coy. I.R. versus C. Coy. R.I.F. at Cappelle result Opale to 4 goals.	
	25th		Battalion Cross Country Run of 3 miles. Divisional Cross Country Run - Team of 8 entered. B. Coy I.R. lecture in Demobilisation. Church Parade Battalion in Brigade Duty for week. 7.O.R.s to Disposal Centre.	
	26th		Dance in Battalion Theatre.	
	27th		A & D Coys amalgamated men known as No.1 Coy No.2 Coy. 2 O.Rs to Disposal Centre. Lieut Deans to Disposal Centre.	

WAR DIARY.

Place.	Date	Hour	Summary of Events and Information.	Remarks and reference to appendices.
CAPPELLE	Jany/19 28th		15. O.R.s to Divisional Centre.	
	29th		Lt. Col. Cave D.S.O. Resumes command of Battalion. 6 O.R.s to Divisional Centre.	
	30th		2 O.R.s to Tournaise A.F.C.	
	31st		Battalion What Drive in Operation Area. Capt. L. Purdie Returns whole at Divl. Rest Camp. Curling match under supervision of Padre ⅔ Field Ambce. TEMPLEUVE.	

O. Cave
LIEUT. COLONEL
Commanding 18th Battn. The Scottish Rifles
3rd February 1919.

99999

18th Scottish Rifles.

War Diary.

1st February to 28th February

1919

SR/102.

Army Form C. 2118.

WAR DIARY
or
INTELLIGENCE SUMMARY.
(Erase heading not required.)

Instructions regarding War Diaries and Intelligence Summaries are contained in F. S. Regs., Part II. and the Staff Manual respectively. Title pages will be prepared in manuscript.

Place	Date 1919	Hour	Summary of Events and Information	Remarks and references to Appendices
Cappell.	Feby. 1st		12 officers to Dispersal Centre. O.R.	
"	2nd	10.00	Farewell performance of Battalion Concert Party. Team of 20 men submitted for Corps Cross Country Run cancelled.	
"	3rd		Church Parade at Theatre. Conference of Company Commanders to decide Cadre. 62 O.R. to Dispersal Centre. 6 Clerks sent to Base Commandant, Etaples. Brigade Duties continued until Wednesday 5th. Prince of Wales to visit Bersee. Captain Watson returns.	
"	4th		Prince of Wales to visit 47th Brigade at Pont a Marq and present colours.	
"	5th		New instructions received regarding Demobilisation of Army. Returns of all men fulfilling necessary conditions rendered by Companies A/R.S.M. McMullan returned to Company. 2nd Lieut.Telfer leaves for Course at Oxford. C.S.M. Cormack becomes A/R.S.M. 2nd Lieut.Kirkwood proceeds on leave. On return to take duties of L/G.Officer to Cadre. 2nd Lieut.Spreckley proceeds on leave to U.K. Heavy fall of snow. Capt.Hamilton and 2nd	
"	6th		Lieut.Hopper take on Company duties. .... Working Parties as usual. Medical Officer goes on leave. Lecture in Theatre by C.O. on "Army of Occupation" Baths and interior economy. Lieut Col. Wilkie returns after three months leave.	
"	7th		20.R. to Dispersal Centre. Selection of names of 10 officers and 200 O.R.for Army of Occupation. Lieut.Dalrymple returns from leave and 2nd Lieut.Beattie from Hospital. Draft for Germany draw clean underclothing at Div.Baths,Templeuve, but Battalion Baths.utilised.	
"	8th		Lt.Col.Wilde resumes command of Battalion. 5 O.R. to Dispersal Centre	
"	9th	10.00	Church Parades. C of E and Pres., in Theatre at 10 .00 hours R.C.at Templeuve. 24 O.R. for Dispersal Centre.	
"	10 th		13 O.R. to Dispersal Centre. Parades P.T. and Education. Start of the new rules re demobilisation i.e.,Long Service, age and wound stripes.	
"	11th		P.T. and Education under Coy arrangements. 2nd Lieut.Mannes M.C. is authorised to wear the badge of rank of Captain whilst acting as Adjutant. Authority Section 1 CMS 384.	
"	12th		Companies march to Templeuve to draw clean clothing. Baths at Cappelle. Lieut.Harper returns from leave.	
"	13th		10 O.R. for Dispersal Centre. 09.00 -1200 hrs Rifle exercise and Education. Lena Ashwells Concert Party Perform at Marie,Templeuve at 17.30 hrs.	
"	14th		6 O.R. to Dispersal Centre. 0800 -1200 hours Rifle Exercise and Education.	
"	15th		Working Parties. Visit of Divisional Commander. 2nd Lieut.Hart returns from leave. Captain Watson and 21 O.R. to Dispersal Centre.	
"	16th	08.00	C.of E. Holy Communion in Recreation Rooms. Other services as usual. 2nd Lieut.Miller returns from leave. 12 O.R. to Dispersal Centre.	

Army Form C. 2118.

WAR DIARY
or
INTELLIGENCE SUMMARY.
(Erase heading not required.)

Instructions regarding War Diaries and Intelligence Summaries are contained in F. S. Regs. Part II. and the Staff Manual respectively. Title pages will be prepared in manuscript.

Place	Date	Hour	Summary of Events and Information	Remarks and references to Appendices
Cappelle	1919 Feby. 17		Working Parties at Templeuve. XXXX 2.O.R. for Dispersal Centre. Board of Enquiry at C.M. Stores for purpose of checking stores.	
"	18		Parades P.T., Rifle Exercises and Education. Football Match at 1400 hrs Officers v Rest of Battalion. Result a draw 3 goals each.	
"	19		9. O.R. for Dispersal Centre. Parades P.T. Rifle Exercises and Education.	
"	20		2. O.R. to Dispersal Centre under Lieut. Beattie, Conducting Officer. Parades P.T., Rifle Exercises and Education. Guard Duties at Templeuve. Dance in Chateau Dupont for officers at 2000 hrs.	
"	21		Guard Duties at Templeuve. Lieut. Kirkwood returns from leave.	
"	22		Guard Duties at Templeuve. 1 Officer and 16 O.R. awarded Parchment Certificates.	
"	23		Guard Duties at Templeuve. Baths at Pont a Marcq for Battalion.	
"	24		Guard Duties at Templeuve. Working Party. 300 French Artillery billetted in Cappelle. Battalion Dinner at Lille for O.Rs night.	
"	25		Guard Duties and Working Parties at Templeuve. "Very Lights" Concert Party visit Templeuve. Major Eaves to Hospital.	
"	26		Guard Duties and Working Party at Templeuve. Football Match 1415 hrs at Templeuve between 112th Field Ambulance and 18th Scottish Rifles. Dance at Chateau Dupont, Cappelle for officers at 20.00 hrs. Divisional General paid Headquarters a visit at 11.00 hrs. 10 Men for Educational Examination.	
"	27		Guard Duties and Working Party at Templeuve. Major Crawford on Special Leave from to-day.	
"	28		Guard Duties and Working Party at Templeuve. 2nd Lieut A.Mc.I.Michie to U.K. sick. R.Q.M.S.Adie to Dispersal Centre.	

[signed]
LIEUT. COLONEL
Commanding 18th Battn. The Scottish Rifles

www.ingramcontent.com/pod-product-compliance
Lightning Source LLC
Chambersburg PA
CBHW081502160426
43193CB00014B/2566